T0061483

THE EASY PIANO COLLECTION
ORCHESTRAL
GOLD

Published by:
Chester Music Limited,
14-15 Berners Street, London W1T 3LJ, UK.

Exclusive Distributors:
Music Sales Limited,
Distribution Centre, Newmarket Road, Bury St Edmunds, Suffolk IP33 3YB, UK.
Music Sales Corporation,
180 Madison Avenue, 24th Floor, New York NY 10016, USA.
Music Sales Pty Limited,
Units 3-4, 17 Willfox Street, Condell Park, NSW 2200, Australia.

Order No. CH81961
ISBN 978-1-78305-442-8
This book © Copyright 2014 by Chester Music.

Edited by Ruth Power.
Foreward by Jonathan Paxman.
CD recorded and produced by Mutual Chord Studio, Guangzhou, China.
CD manufactured and book printed in the EU.

Your Guarantee of Quality:
As publishers, we strive to produce every book to the highest commercial standards.
The music has been freshly engraved and carefully designed to minimise
awkward page turns to make playing from it a real pleasure.
Particular care has been given to specifying acid-free, neutral-sized
paper made from pulps which have not been elemental chlorine bleached.
This pulp is from farmed sustainable forests and was produced
with special regard for the environment.
Throughout, the printing and binding have been planned to ensure a sturdy,
attractive publication which should give years of enjoyment.
If your copy fails to meet our high standards, please inform us and we will gladly replace it.

www.musicsales.com

CHESTER MUSIC
part of The Music Sales Group

London/New York/Paris/Sydney/Copenhagen/Berlin/Madrid/Hong Kong/Tokyo

The Easy Piano Collection Orchestral Gold

Chester Music's *The Easy Piano Collection Orchestral Gold* presents accessible transcriptions of some of the world's greatest and best-loved concert music. The pieces themselves derive from an extensive range of instrumental genres, including suite and sinfonia, concerto grosso and solo concerto, serenade, march, overture and symphony.

Typifying the glories of the Baroque style are Vivaldi, Bach and Handel. From Antonio Vivaldi, an Italian composer of nearly 500 concertos, comes the dreamy 'Largo' (second movement) from *Spring*, the first concerto of the celebrated *Four Seasons*. Vivaldi's influence was far-reaching and extended to the great Johann Sebastian Bach, who made keyboard transcriptions of some of Vivaldi's earlier, ground-breaking concertos. Bach himself wrote one of the greatest Baroque concerto collections, the *Brandenburg* Concertos, completed in 1721. The appellation would have probably annoyed Bach, since Margrave Christian Ludwig of Brandenburg, to whom the concertos were dedicated, ignored them entirely (possibly because they were unsuited to his small resident ensemble). In addition to the 'Adagio' from *Brandenburg* Concerto No. 6, this collection presents what is perhaps Bach's most widely-recognised instrumental piece, 'Air on the G String', from the Orchestral Suite No. 3 (1731).

A second 'Air' included in this collection comes from George Frideric Handel's *Water Music* suite (1717), which enjoyed a much happier reception than Bach's 'Brandenburgs'. It was written for King George I and performed by 50 musicians on a large barge on the River Thames in London. The king relished the music and ordered an immediate repeat performance. By contrast, Handel's *Music For the Royal Fireworks*, from which *Orchestral Gold* presents the triumphant 'La Réjouissance', experienced near-humiliation at its first performance. The fireworks at the 1749 première in London's Green Park not only failed to work as planned, they also set fire to the enormous wooden palace-cum-launch-pad constructed for the event.

The Classical-era music of this collection spotlights three more great composers: Haydn, Mozart and Beethoven. From Joseph Haydn comes an elegant theme that opens the second movement 'Andante' of the *London* Symphony, No. 104. This was the crowing work of two sets of six symphonies Haydn composed for London during the years 1791–95.

Haydn's music, his pioneering quartets and symphonies especially, had a profound influence on Wolfgang Amadeus Mozart. *Orchestral Gold* extracts music from Mozart's final two symphonic masterpieces, the first movement theme of No. 40 in G Minor, and the third movement Minuet from No. 41 in C Major. Also included is the sublime 'Adagio' second movement from the Clarinet Concerto in A Major, which Mozart completed just weeks before his death in December 1791.

The symphonies of Ludwig van Beethoven broke new ground for the genre. Both the Third (1803) and Fifth (1808) symphonies convey triumph over adversity and look forward to the Romantic era in their subjective and visionary spirit. The Sixth 'Pastoral' Symphony is likewise a highly subjective composition, but here we find Beethoven's heartfelt response to the wonders of nature. Following a fourth-movement depiction of a violent storm, the theme of the fifth and final movement, presented in this collection, represents a folksong of thanksgiving.

Felix Mendelssohn wrote five numbered symphonies, the most popular of them the Third (Scottish) and Fourth (*Italian*). The *Scottish* was begun in 1829 during a visit to the ruined chapel of Holyrood Castle in Edinburgh. The piece is characterised by song-like themes, and it is the first movement's opening 'Andante' presented here, in all its melancholic beauty.

Mendelsohn was among the many Romantics drawn to programmatic music, where pictures, stories and other extra-musical ideas stimulate the compositional process. We find this in Modest Mussorgsky's *Pictures at an Exhibition* (1874), a work originally written for piano, and only orchestrated after the composer's death. Pyotr Ilyich Tchaikovsky took a subtle and very personal programmatic approach in his Fifth and Sixth symphonies (1888, 1893), although by way of contrast *Orchestral Gold* includes the same composer's pounding 1812 Overture (best played when the neighbours are out) and the sensuous woodwind theme from the *Romeo and Juliet* Fantasy Overture.

Edward Elgar's music straddles the 19th and 20th centuries. The charming *Salut D'Amour* (1888) bought him wide attention from the public, and with the *Enigma Variations* (1899) he established himself as the leading English composer of the age. Creeping into the 20th century, this collection presents the noble, patriotic side of Elgar with the hymnal 'Land of Hope and Glory' (from *Pomp and Circumstance* March No. 1) and an extract from the spirited *Cockaigne* Overture (both 1901).

It is worth noting that piano transcriptions of concert music have a highly respectable history: such luminaries as Bach, Liszt and Brahms indulged in this very practice. It allows the composer's orchestral inspiration and invention to be appreciated through music making in the home. This is indeed the very purpose of *The Easy Piano Collection Orchestral Gold*, a magnificent compilation of inspiring music to play and enjoy.

Jonathan Paxman

1812 Overture
(Op.49)

Composed by Pyotr Ilyich Tchaikovksy

Largo

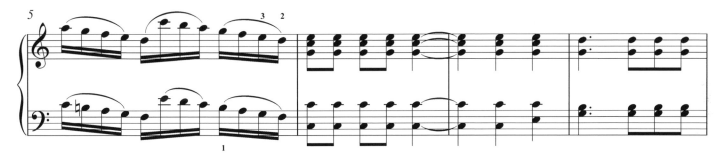

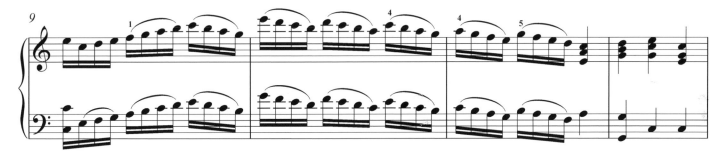

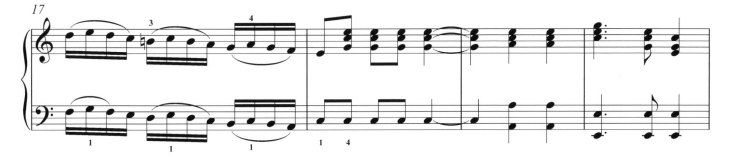

Allegro vivace

Air
(from 'Water Music')

Composed by George Frideric Handel

Largo

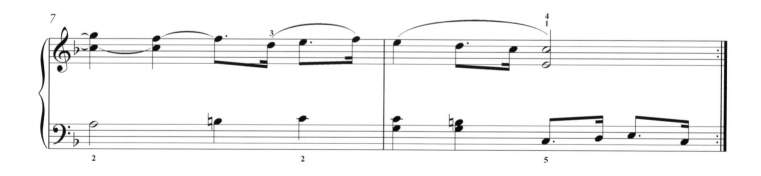

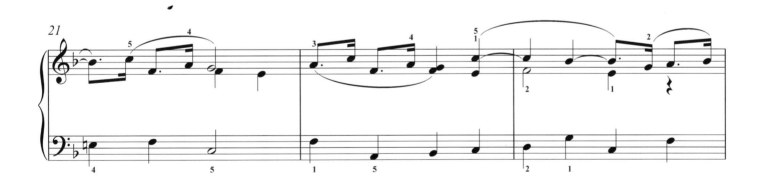

molto rit.

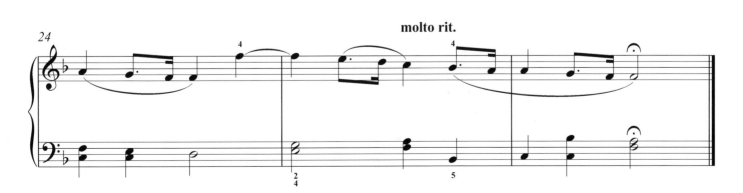

9

Air On The G String
(from 'Suite No.3')

Composed by Johann Sebastian Bach

Lento, espressivo

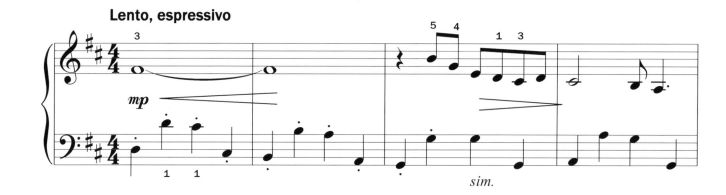

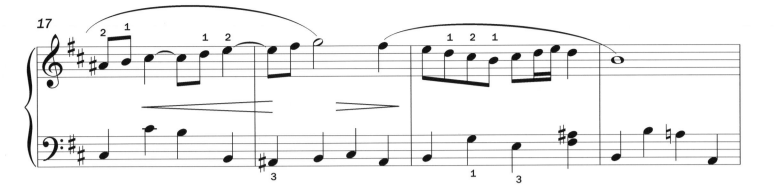

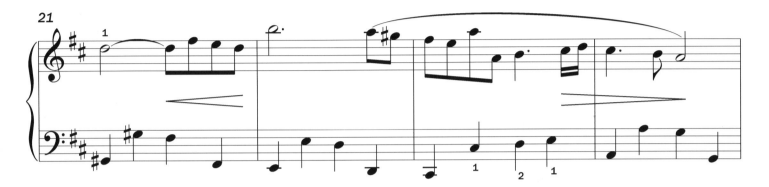

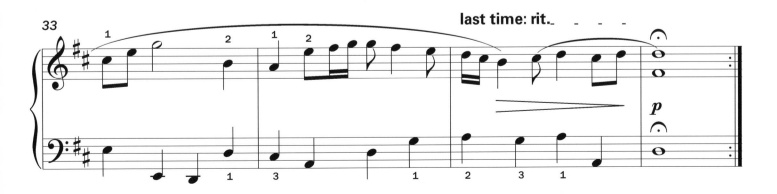

The Arrival of the Queen of Sheba
(from 'Solomon')

Composed by George Frideric Handel

Allegro

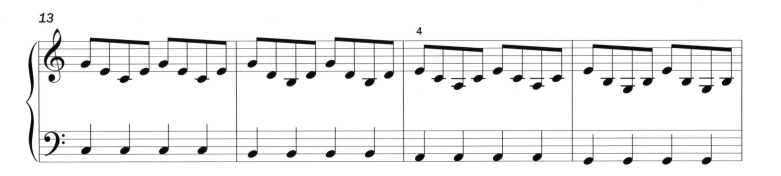

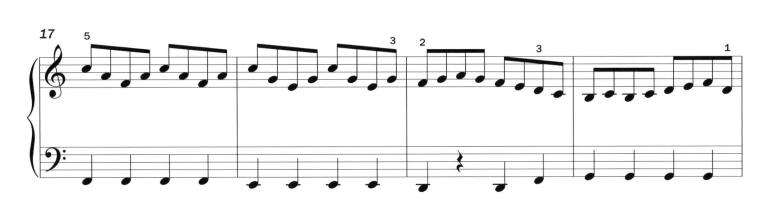

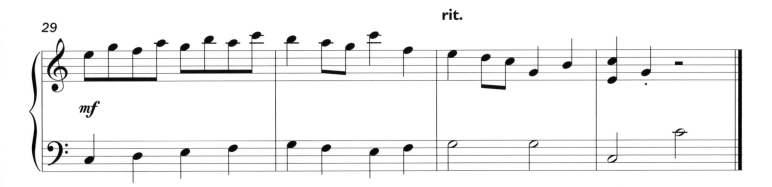

Badinerie
(from 'Orchestral Suite No.2')

Composed by Johann Sebastian Bach

Allegro

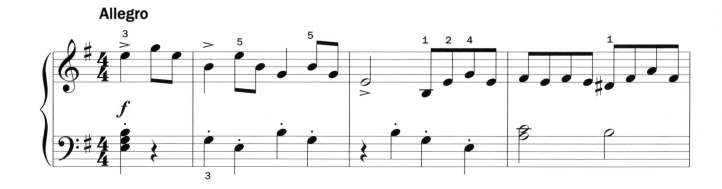

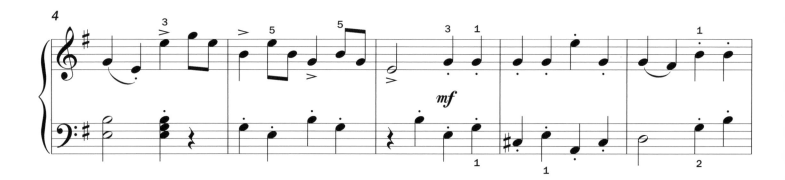

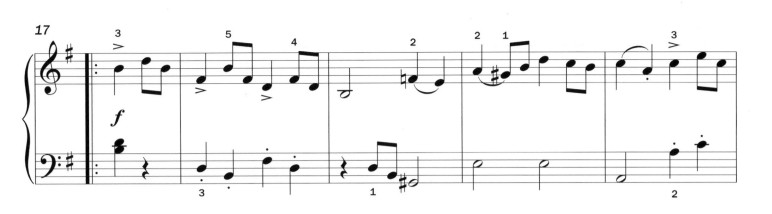

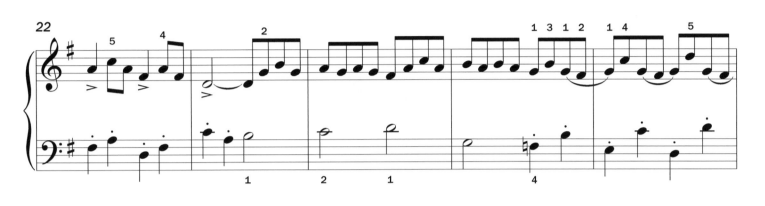

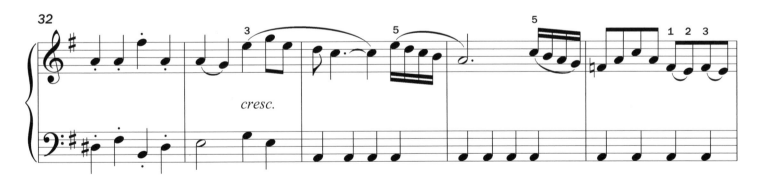

Brandenburg Concerto No.6
(2nd movement: Adagio, ma non tanto)

Composed by Johann Sebastian Bach

Adagio, ma non tanto

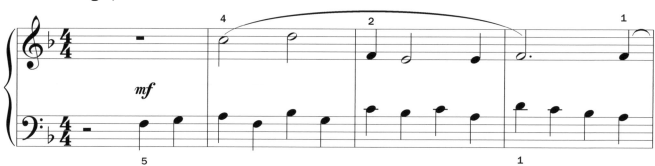

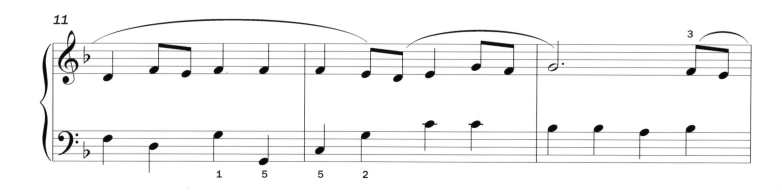

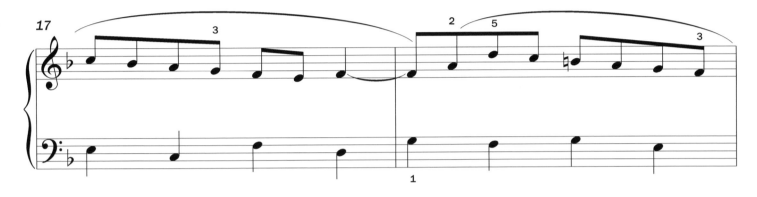

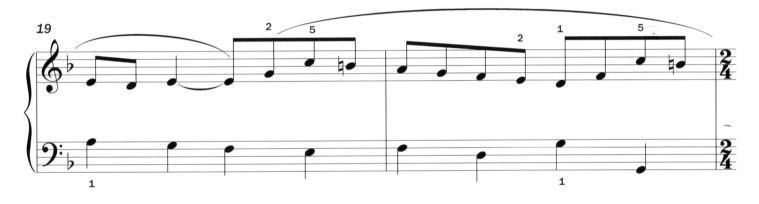

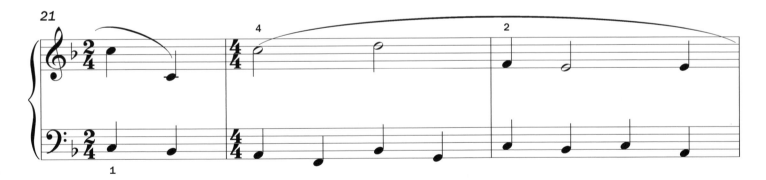

rit.

Clarinet Concerto in A major
K622 (2nd movement: Adagio)

Composed by Wolfgang Amadeus Mozart

Adagio

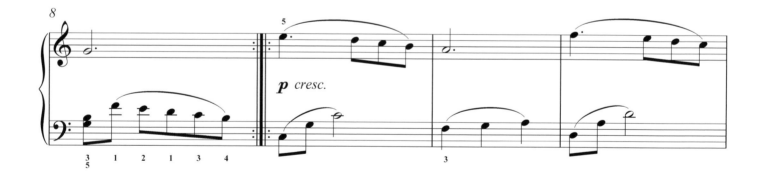

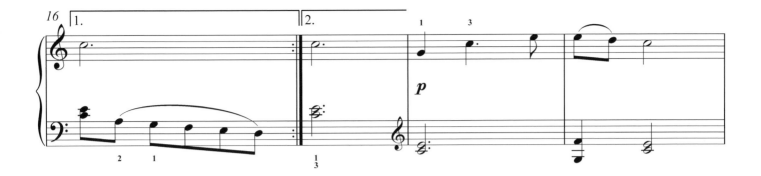

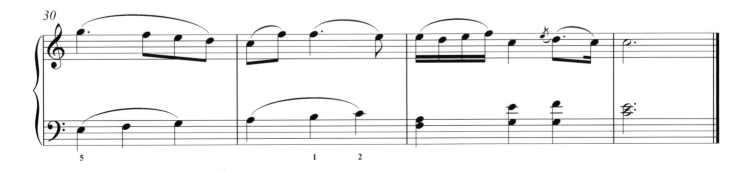

Eine Kleine Nachtmusik
K525 (1st movement theme)

Composed by Wolfgang Amadeus Mozart

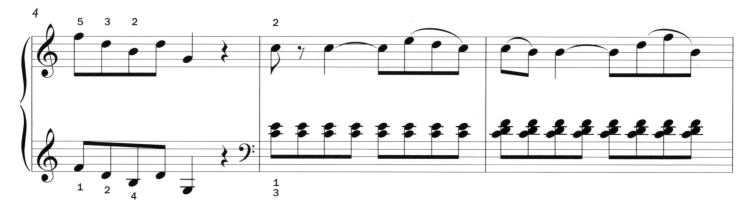

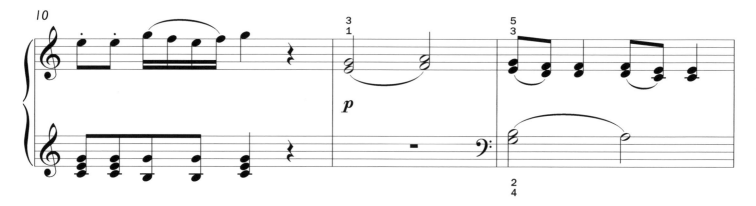

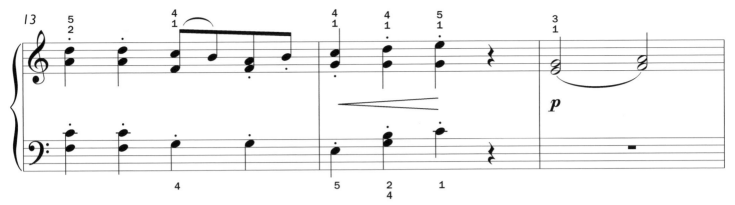

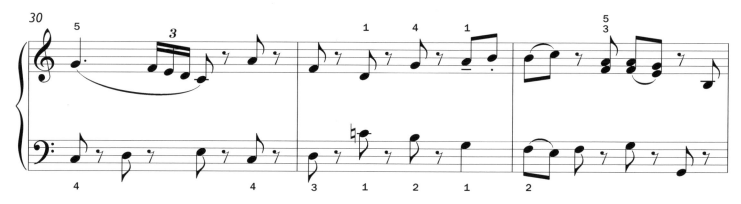

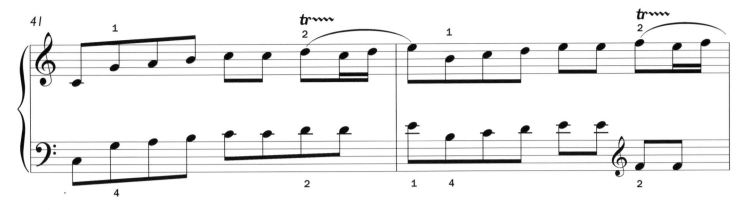

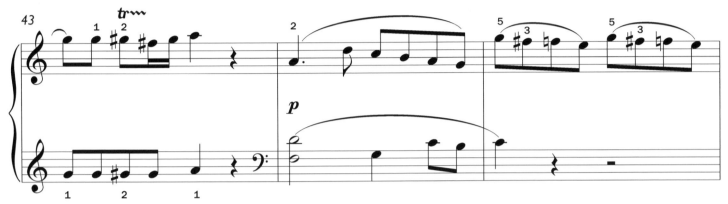

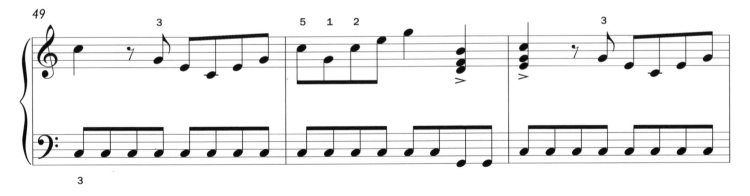

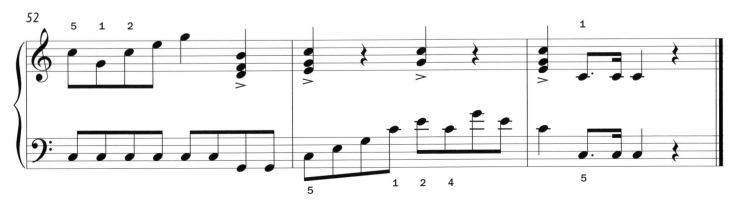

Enigma Variations, Op.36
(Theme)

Composed by Edward Elgar

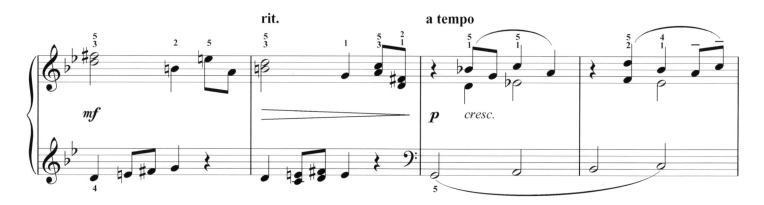

Hornpipe
(from 'Water Music')

Composed by George Frideric Handel

Brightly

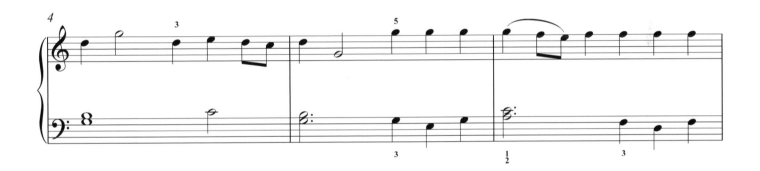

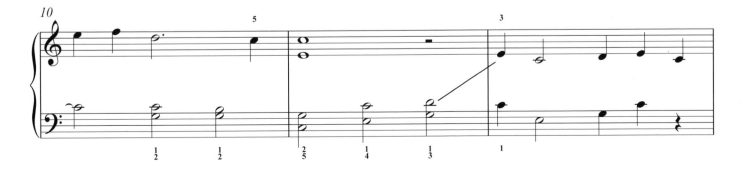

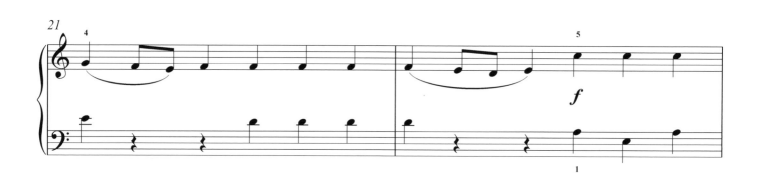

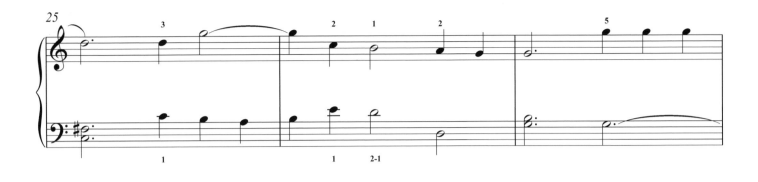

rall.

La Réjouissance
(from 'Music For The Royal Fireworks')

Composed by George Frideric Handel

rit.

Cockaigne Overture, Op.40
(Extract)

Composed by Edward Elgar

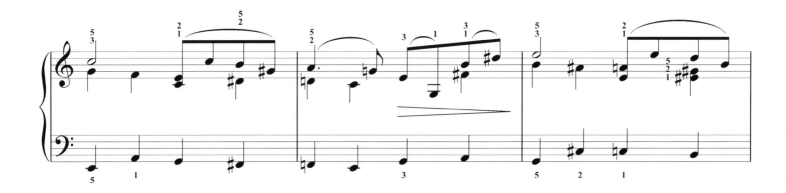

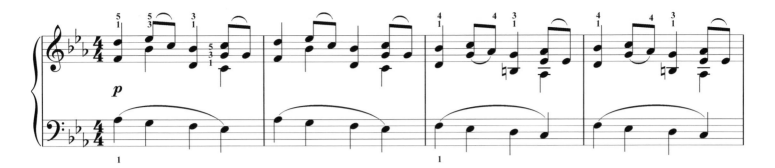

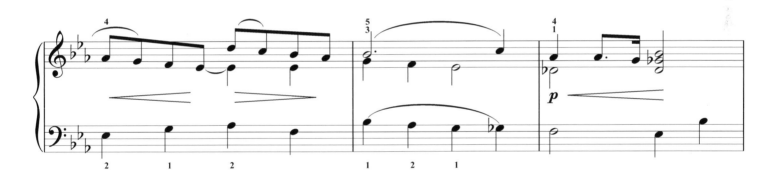

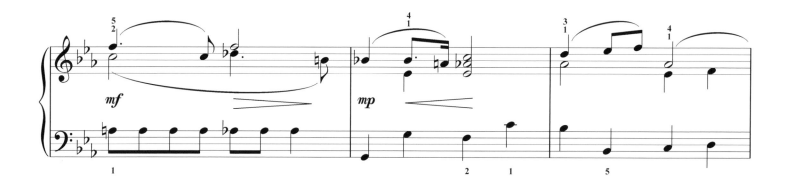

Land Of Hope And Glory
(Pomp and Circumstance March No.1)

Composed by Edward Elgar

Largamente

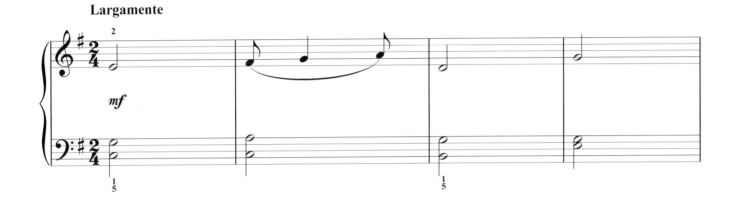

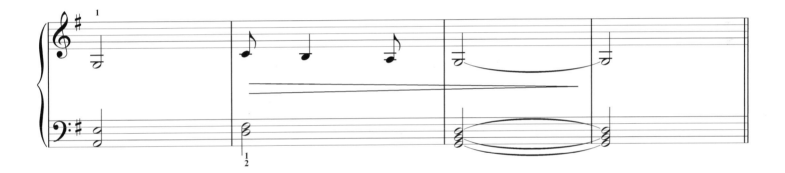

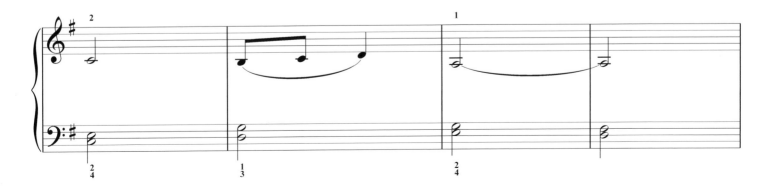

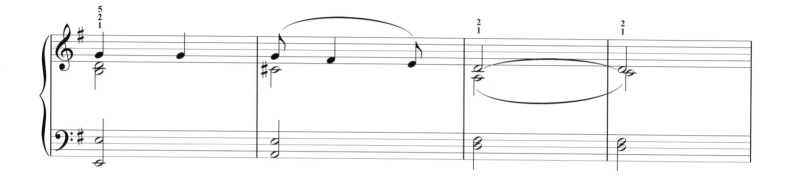

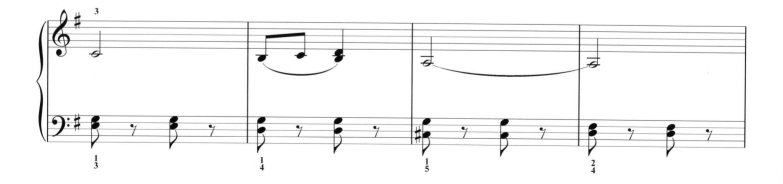

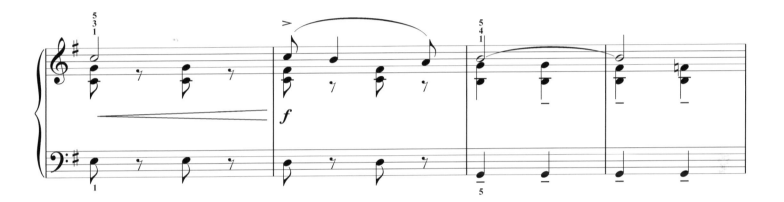

Promenade
(from 'Pictures At An Exhibtion')

Composed by Modest Mussorgsky

Allegro giusto, nel modo Russico, senza allegreza, ma poco sostenuto

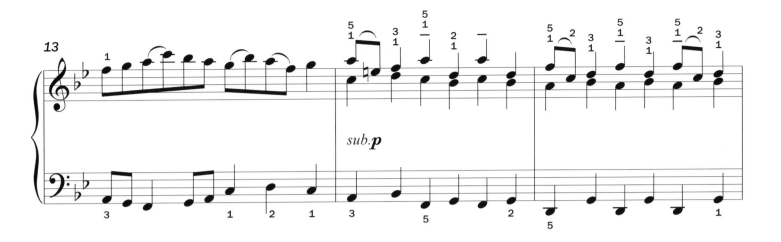

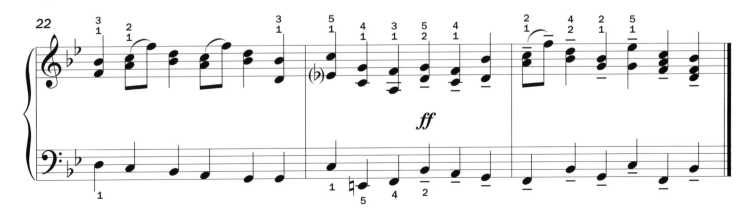

Romeo And Juliet
(Fantasy Overture)

Composed by Pyotr Ilyich Tchaikovsky

Moderato espressivo

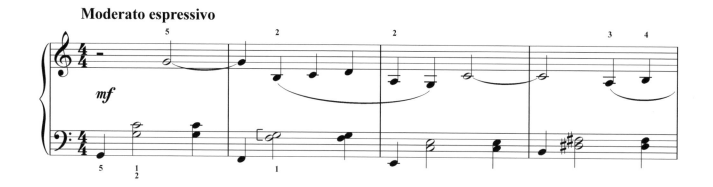

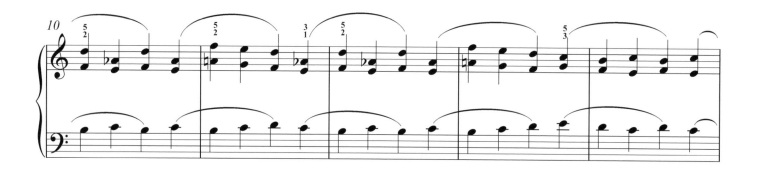

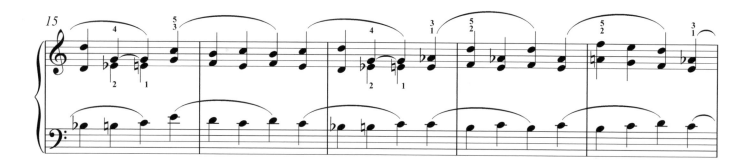

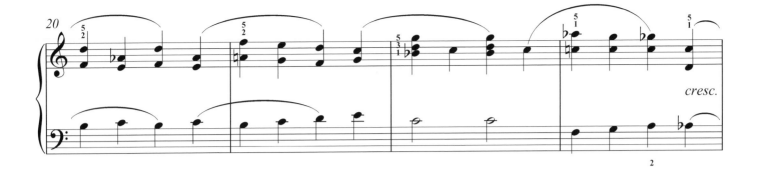

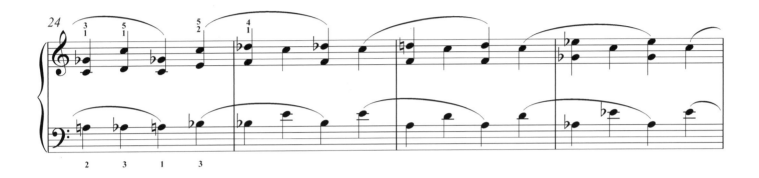

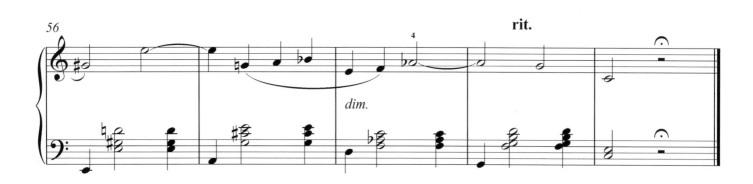

Symphony No.3 'Scottish'
(1st movement theme)

Composed by Felix Mendelssohn

Andante con moto

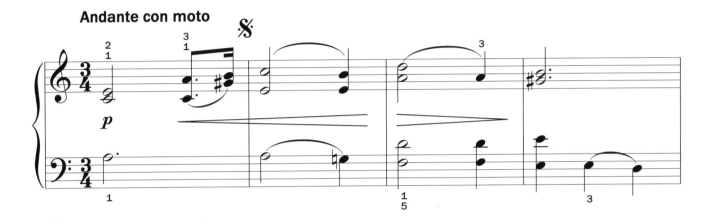

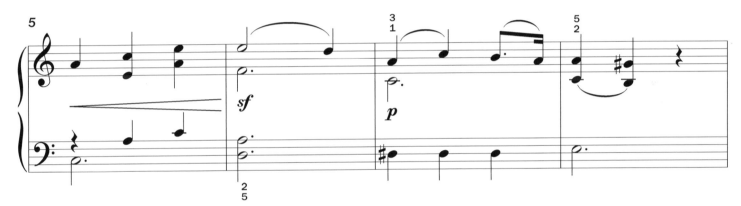

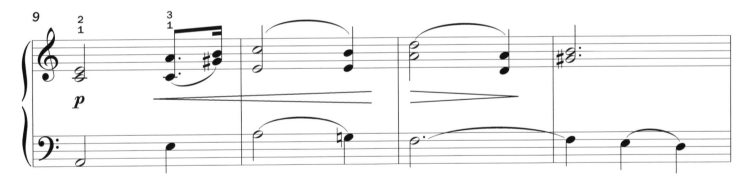

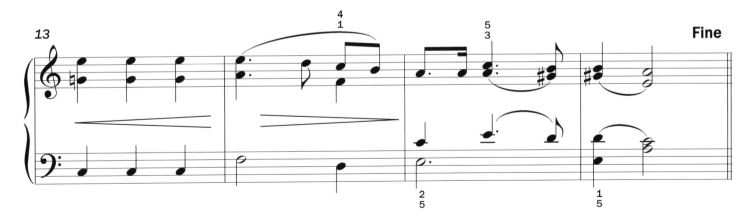

Allegro un poco agitato

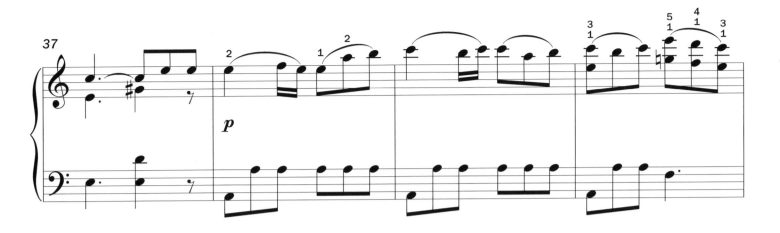

Tempo primo

D.S. al Fine

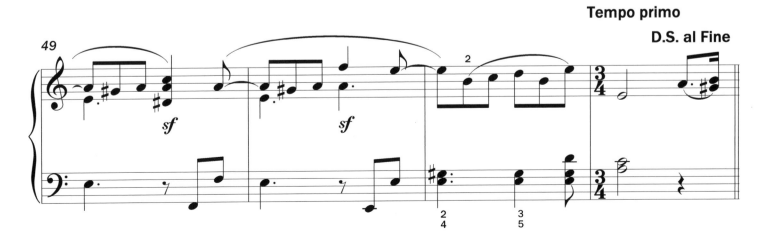

Salut d'amour, Op.12

Composed by Edward Elgar

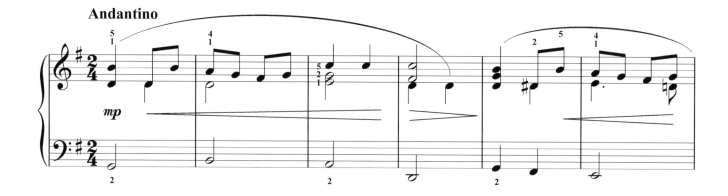

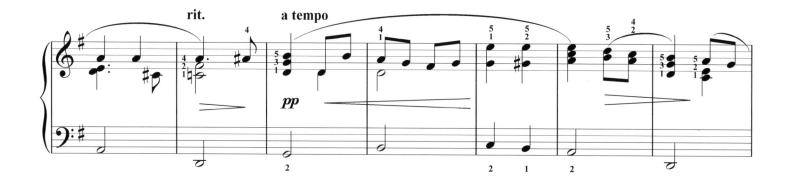

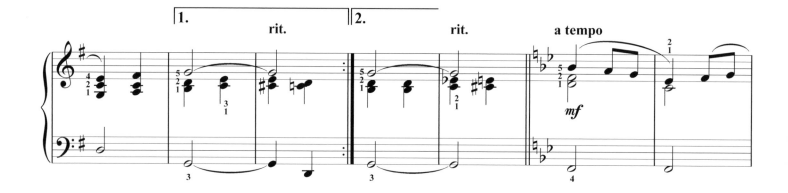

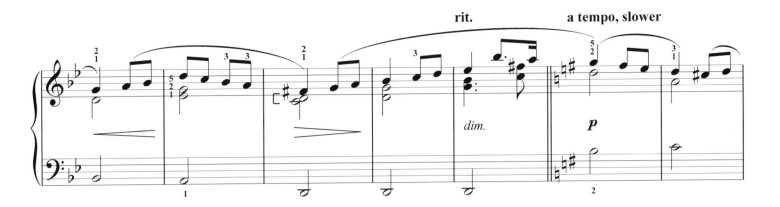

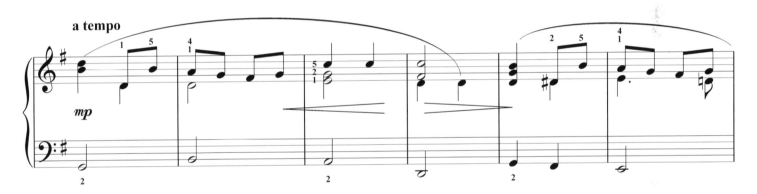

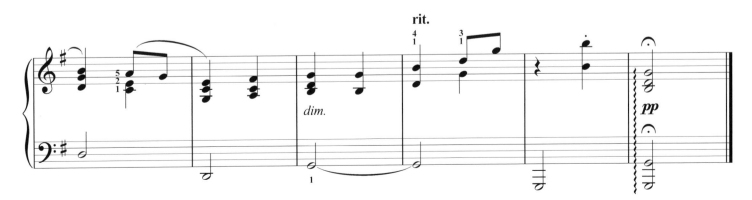

Spring (2nd movement)
(from 'The Four Seasons')

Composed by Antonio Vivaldi

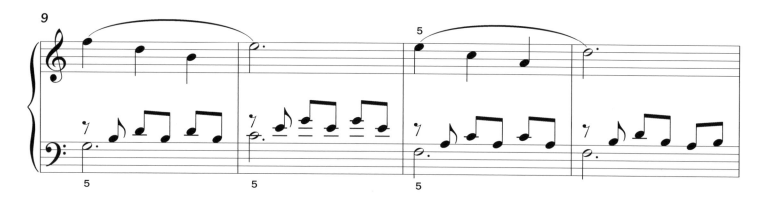

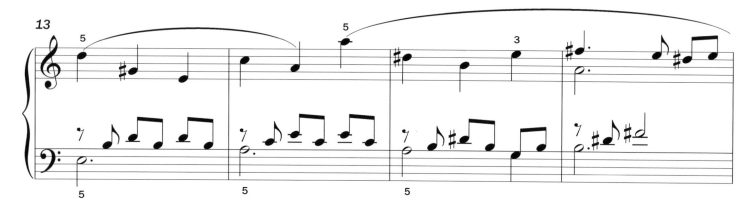

molto rit.

Symphony No.104 'London'
(2nd movement: Andante)

Composed by Franz Joseph Haydn

Andante

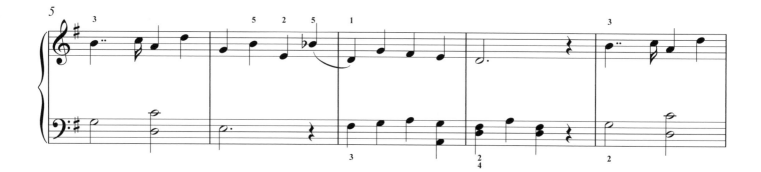

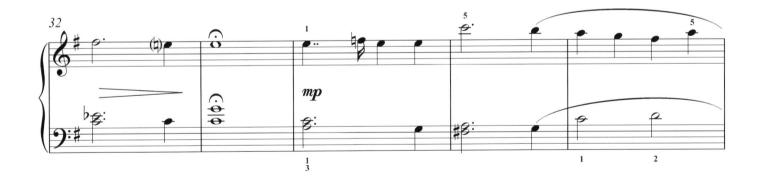

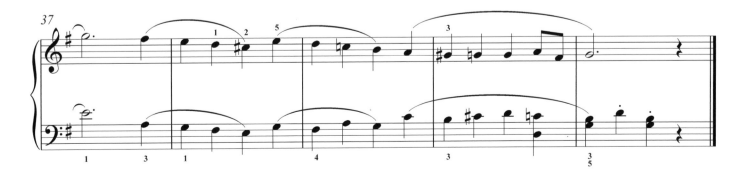

Symphony No.40 in G minor
K550 (1st movement: Molto Allegro)

Composed by Wolfgang Amadeus Mozart

Allegro molto

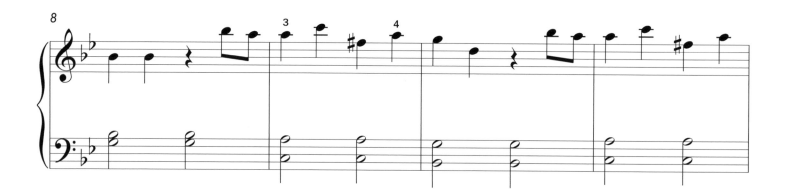

Symphony No.41 'Jupiter'
K551 (3rd movement: Minuet)

Composed by Wolfgang Amadeus Mozart

Allegretto

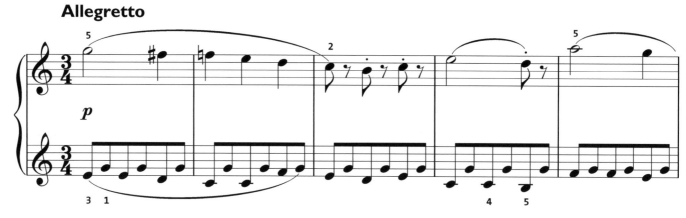

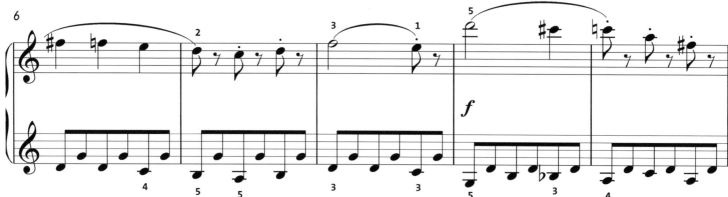

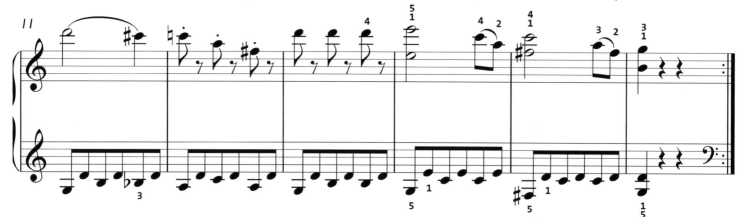

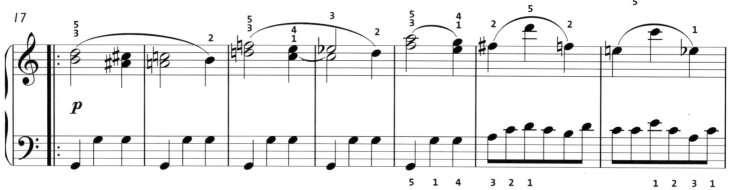

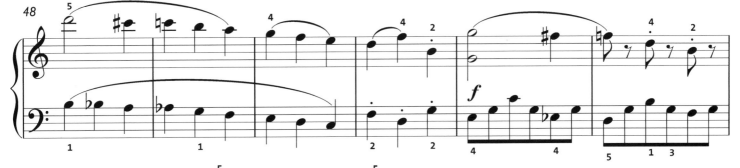

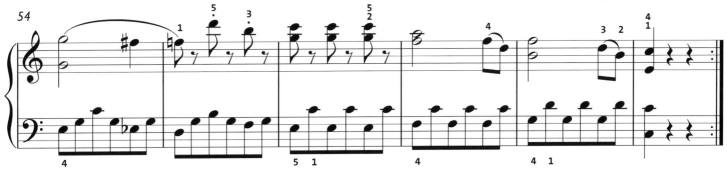

Symphony No.3 'Eroica'
Op.55 (Theme)

Composed by Ludwig van Beethoven

Allegro con brio

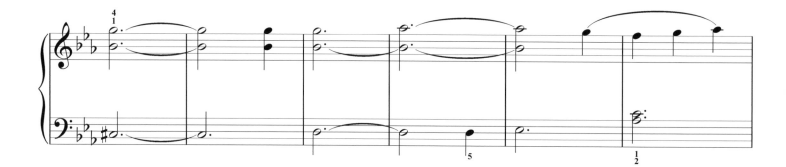

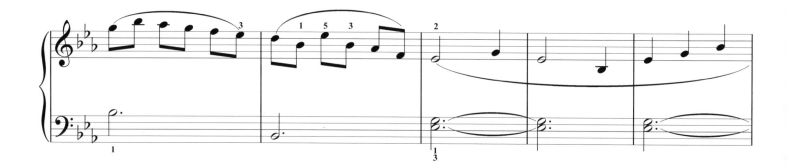

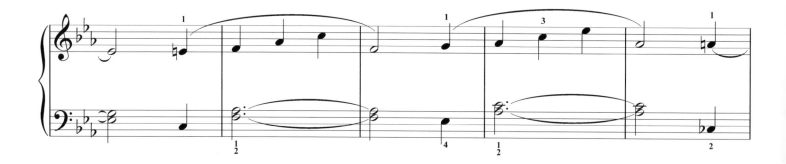

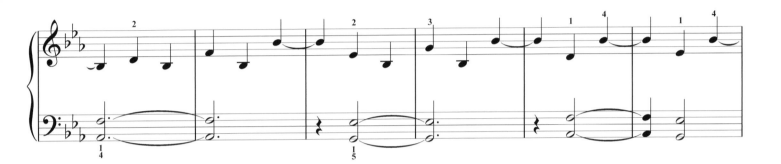

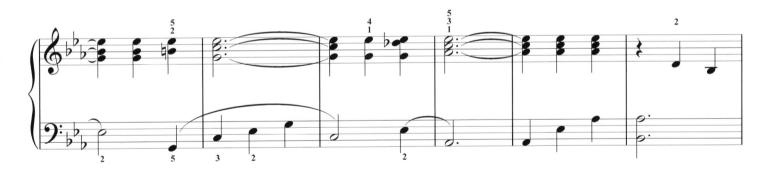

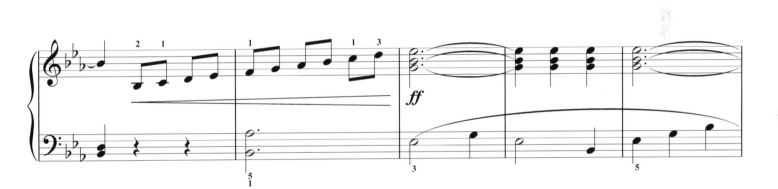

Symphony No.5 in E minor, Op.64
(Andante cantabile theme)

Composed by Pyotr Ilyich Tchaikovsky

Andante cantabile

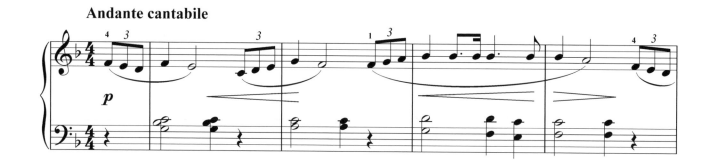

Symphony No.5
Op.67 (1st movement)

Composed by Ludwig van Beethoven

Allegro

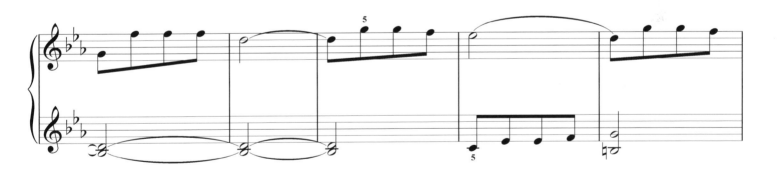

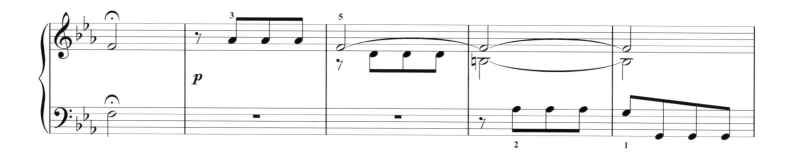

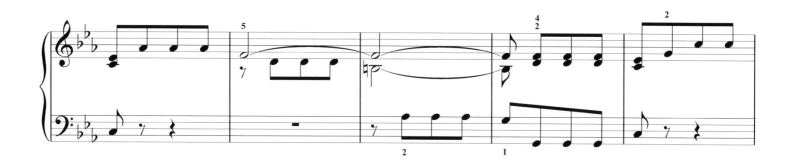

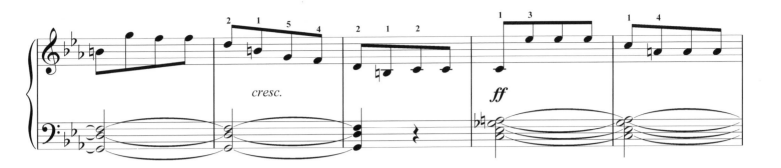

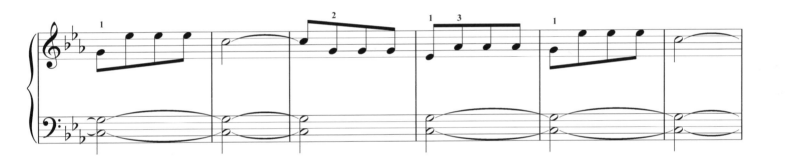

Symphony No.6 'Pathétique', Op.74
(1st movement)

Composed by Pyotr Ilyich Tchaikovsky

Andante

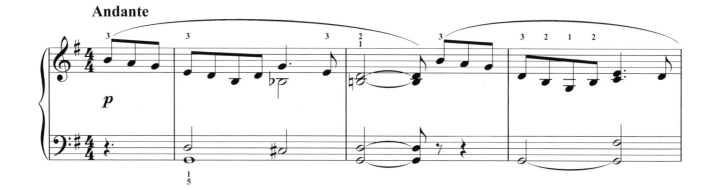

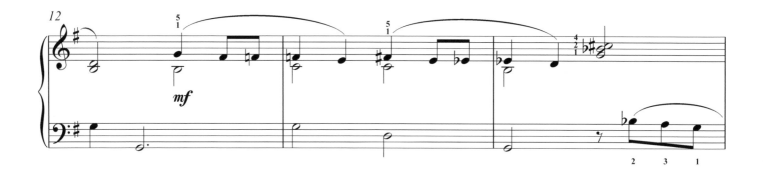

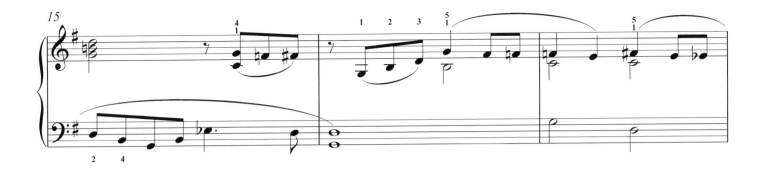

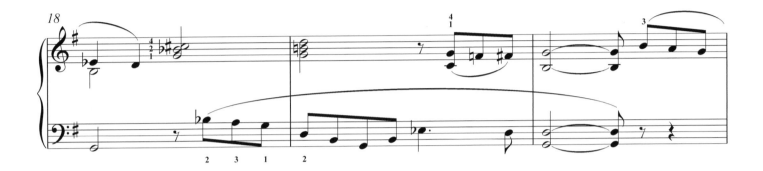

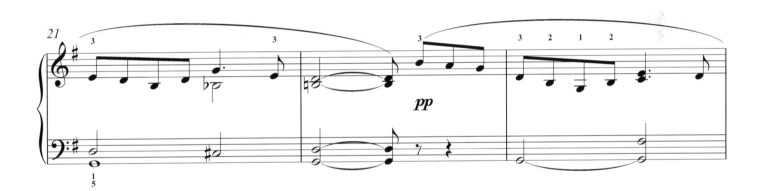

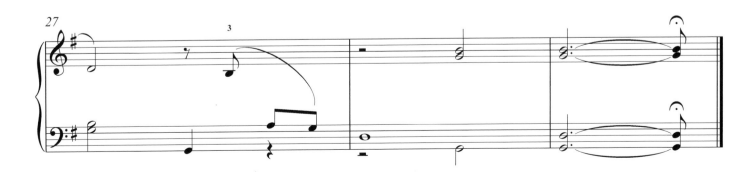

Symphony No.6 'Pastoral'
Op.68 (5th movement)

Composed by Ludwig van Beethoven

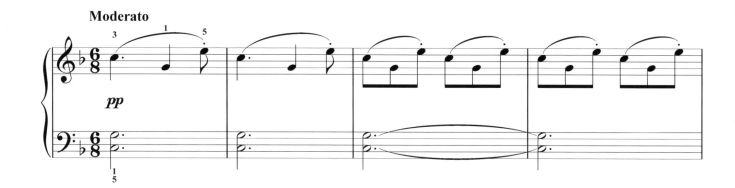

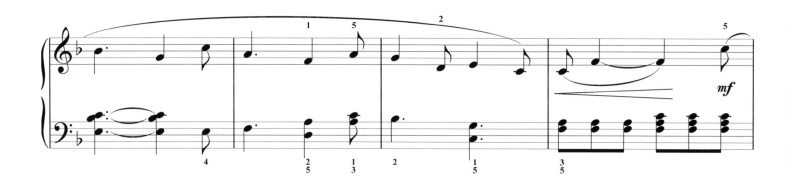

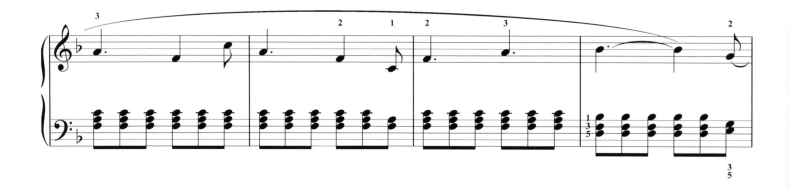

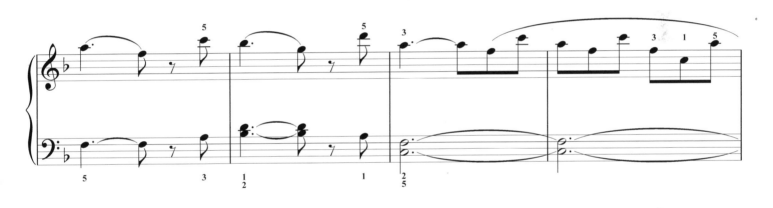

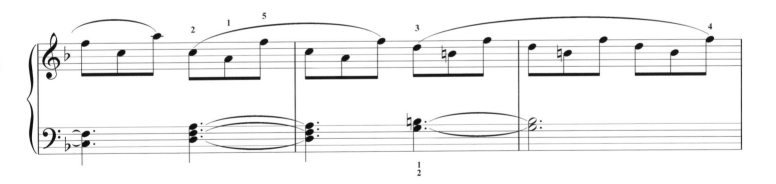

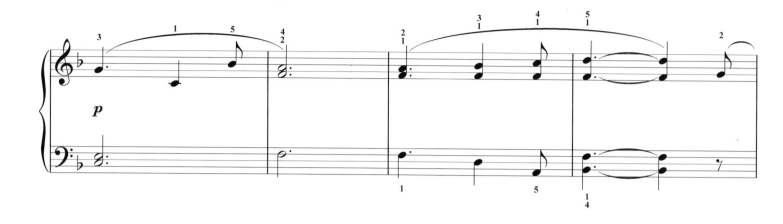

23456789